RAILWAY HISTORY IN PICTURES:
THE STOCKTON & DARLINGTON RAILWAY

Railway history in pictures series
Midlands by H. C. Casserley and C. C. Dorman
North-East England by K. Hoole
North-West England by J. A. Patmore and J. Clark
Wales and the Welsh Border Counties by H. C. Casserley
The West Country by R. C. Riley
Ireland Vols 1 and 2 by A. MacCutcheon
Scottish by John Thomas
The Somerset & Dorset Railway by Robin Atthill

RAILWAY HISTORY IN PICTURES

The Stockton & Darlington Railway

K. HOOLE

DAVID & CHARLES

NEWTON ABBOT LONDON NORTH POMFRET (VT) VANCOUVER

0 7153 6770 6

© K. Hoole 1975

Set in 11/13-pt. Baskerville
by Wordsworth (Typesetting) Limited
and printed in Great Britain
by Compton Printing Ltd.
Aylesbury, England.
for David & Charles (Holdings) Limited
South Devon House   Newton Abbot   Devon

Published in the United States of America
by David & Charles Inc   North Pomfret
Vermont 05053   USA

Published in Canada by Douglas David &
Charles Limited   3645 McKechnie Drive
West Vancouver BC

LIST OF ILLUSTRATIONS

LIST OF ILLUSTRATIONS

LIST OF ILLUSTRATIONS

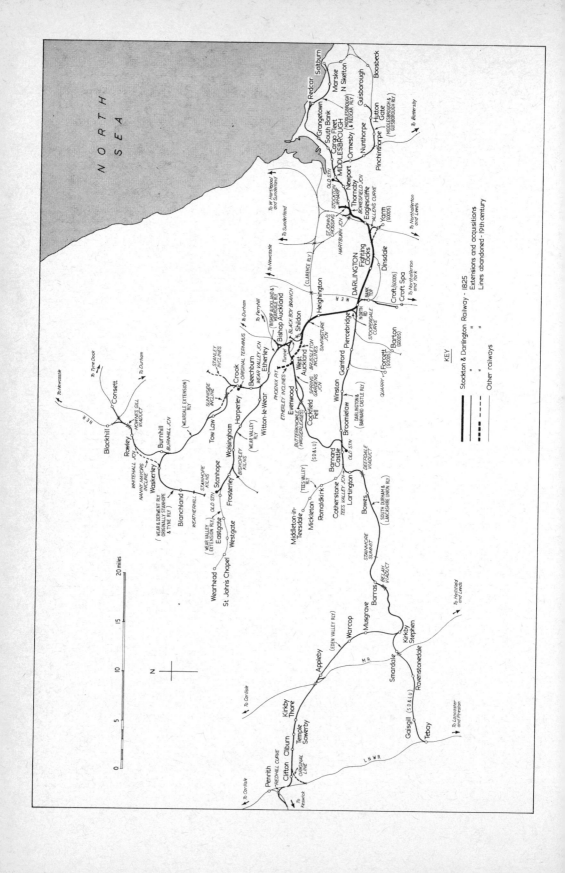

NORTH SEA

Soltburn
Redcar
Marske
N Skelton
Guisborough
Boosbeck
Grangetown
South Bank
Cargo Fleet (MIDDLESBROUGH & REDCAR RLY)
MIDDLESBROUGH
Ormesby
Nunthorpe
Hutton Gate
Pinchinthorpe (MIDDLESBROUGH & GUISBOROUGH RLY)
To Battersby
OLD STN
STOCKTON WHARF
Newport
BOWESFIELD JCN
Thornaby
Eaglescliffe
ALLEN'S CURVE
Yarm (GOODS)
To Northallerton and Leeds
ST JOHN'S CROSSING
HARTBURN JCN
To W Hartlepool and Sunderland
To Sunderland
Fighting Cocks
Dinsdale
DARLINGTON
BANK TOP
Croft (GOODS)
Croft Spa
To Northallerton and York
To Newcastle
(CLARENCE RLY)
NORTH RD
STOCKPERDALE CURVE
Heighington
Barton (GOODS)
(FERRYHILL)
To Ferryhill
To Durham
Shildon
West Auckland
Bishop Auckland
SIMPASTURE JCN
BLACK BOY BRANCH
BROSSLETON INCLINES
Forcett (GOODS)
QUARRY
Piercebridge
Winston
Gainford
Broomielaw
Barnard Castle
OLD STN
(SOUTH DURHAM & LANCASHIRE UNION RLY)
DARLINGTON & BARNARD CASTLE RLY
TEES VALLEY JCN
Cotherstone
Lartington
Bowes
DEEPDALE VIADUCT
Mickleton
Romaldkirk
(TEES VALLEY RLY)
Middleton-in-Teesdale
BOWES JCN (S.D.& L.U.)
SPRING GARDENS
Evenwood
Cockfield Fell
PHOENIX PIT
Tunnel
ETHERLEY INCLINES
BUTTERKNOWLE (HAGGERLEASES)
BISHOP AUCKLAND & WEARDALE RLY
ORIGINAL TERMINUS
Etherley
WEAR VALLEY JCN
Beechburn
Crook
SUNNISIDE INCLINE
STANLEY INCLINES
Harperley
Tow Law
Witton-le-Wear
(WEAR VALLEY RLY)
BISHOPLEY KILNS
Wolsingham
Frosterley
Stanhope
OLD STN
STANHOPE KILNS
Eastgate
Westgate
St John's Chapel
Wearhead
(WEAR VALLEY EXTENSION RLY)
(WEAR & DERWENT RLY ORIGINALLY STANHOPE & TYNE RLY)
WEATHERHILL
Blanchland
NANNY MAYORS INCLINE
WHITEHALL JCN
Waskerley
Rowley
BURNHILL JCN
Burnhill
HOWNES GILL VIADUCT
Consett
Blackhill
To Newcastle
To Durham
To Tyne Dock
N.E.R.

Penrith
FREDHALL CURVE
Clifton
Cliburn
Temple Sowerby
ORIGINAL LINE
Kirkby Thore
Appleby
(EDEN VALLEY RLY)
Warcop
Musgrave
Barras
STAINMORE SUMMIT
BELAH VIADUCT
Kirkby Stephen
M R
Smardale
Ravenstonedale
Gaisgill (S.D.& L.U.)
Tebay
L N W R
To Carlisle
To Keswick
To Hellifield and Leeds
To Lancaster and Preston

0 5 10 15 20 miles

N

KEY

Stockton & Darlington Railway - 1825
Extensions and acquisitions
Lines abandoned - 19th century
Other railways

A century and a half of the
Stockton & Darlington Railway

The Stockton & Darlington Railway was the first steam operated public railway in the world when it opened on 27 September 1825. Many railways and wagonways were in existence before that date and for some years a few of these had been worked by steam locomotives. However, the locomotive operated systems were invariably for carrying minerals—usually coal—from the pit-head to the nearest navigable waterway, or point of sale, and thus they were not public carriers. The S & D envisaged its role as a carrier of coal (and other goods) for anyone prepared to pay the relevant haulage charges or tolls. From the beginning the company was allowed to carry traffic in its own wagons, or to haul wagons owned by other companies or individuals, a condition of the latter being that 'the Name or Names and Number' should be painted on the outside of every wagon in large white capital letters (not less than 3in high) on a black ground. In addition each wagon used on the line had to be registered with the railway company, together with the name and address of the owner.

The main object of the S & D was to convey coal from the small pits in west Durham to the River Tees at Stockton for shipment. The original proposal was for a canal and, in fact, a survey was carried out in 1768, although the canal would not have actually reached the pits, passing about four miles to the south of them at Winston. A feature of the proposed canal was that it was to have had three branches, all running south from the main canal, to serve Piercebridge, Croft and Yarm, and the last two were actually built as railway branches some fifty-seven years later.

The first mention of a railway came at a meeting held in Stockton on 18 September 1810, but it was only part of a suggestion for improved transport facilities and called for a railway *or* a canal. Even the Committee appointed to look into the possibilities could not decide which to adopt, but after a survey had been carried out by Rennie he reported in August 1813 in favour of a canal. A further survey for a canal was performed by Leather in 1818, financed by Christopher Tennant.

As with his later scheme, the Clarence Railway, Tennant's preference was for a route avoiding Darlington and naturally his plan was strongly supported by the inhabitants of Stockton. Yarm and Darlington felt that they could not be left out in the cold, with neither canal nor railway, and an approach was made to George Overton, asking him to carry out yet another survey, this time with a railway in view, and yet not entirely abandoning the idea of a canal. It was preferred, of course, that whichever mode of transport was decided upon would serve Darlington and Yarm. Overton found that there was a suitable course for a railway from Stockton to Etherley, and his estimate for thirty-five miles of main line, and eight branches totalling sixteen miles, was £124,000.

In order to meet the Parliamentary deadline for the 1818–19 session plans were hurriedly prepared and deposited, but there was still some uncertainty in the minds of some members of the Committee and the idea of a canal was not entirely abandoned. However, the Bill seeking powers to build a railway was pushed forward, but it was eventually rejected, partly due to the incomplete state of the deposited plans.

Robert Stevenson, the engineer responsible for the Bell Rock lighthouse, also reported on the line and examined Overton's survey, suggesting yet another route but finally, in 1821, after the first Act had been obtained, George Stephenson was brought in by Edward Pease. Pease belonged to a Darlington Quaker family and naturally preferred a line through Darlington, but he wished to confirm Overton's line as a practical proposition. This Stephenson did, except for certain alterations to make the line suitable for locomotives, although their use was nowhere near decided upon. However, when the Bill for the diversions was brought before Parliament in the 1822–3 session it sought powers 'to make and erect such and so many locomotive Engines, as the said Company of Proprietors shall from time to time think proper and expedient, and to use and employ the same in or upon the said Railways or Tramroads'.

Work on the line (under the powers of the 1821 Act) had commenced on 13 May 1822, and ten days later a formal rail laying ceremony was held at St John's Crossing Stockton, but it was another year before Stephenson's deviations were authorised.

The S & D was eventually opened from Witton Park, some five miles north west of Shildon, to Stockton, a total distance of twenty-five miles, and thus Darlington was not the western terminus, as is implied in the title of the company. The first train was worked by the engine delivered by Robert Stephenson & Co, which was later named *Locomotion*. For the first few weeks this was the only locomotive available.

The main centre of operations was Shildon: Darlington and Stockton were of little importance in S & D eyes. The coal was mined near Shildon, the engines and their crews were based at Shildon, and the engines, wagons, coaches and other equipment were all overhauled at Shildon. It was not until some thirty years after the opening of the line that the decision to concentrate the locomotive headquarters at Darlington brought the town into greater prominence. At the eastern end of the line the main centre of industry was moving from Stockton to Middlesbrough, largely because of the new dock, the finding of iron ore in the nearby Eston Hills, and the establishment of several ironworks in the town.

Over the years the S & D was gradually hemmed in by competing lines. The North Eastern was the biggest rival, but there was the Clarence Railway, the West Hartlepool Harbour & Railway, and the Cleveland Railway to contend with, all of which, together with the S & D, fell into the North Eastern's net in the 1860s. However, the former S & D lines continued to be run by a Darlington Committee, which changed things as little as possible. The only control exercised by the NER was on large expenditure. This state of affairs lasted until 1876 when, largely due to the death of William Bouch, the Darlington Committee ceased to exist. Even so the former S & D lines continued to be known and run as the Central Division of the NER, perpetuating some of the practices handed down from the S & D, and it was not until the twentieth century that some departments of the NER abolished the Central Division. Even so, in the 1970s, it is still possible to pick out a few Central Division features here and there in the way of signal boxes, buildings etc.

Little in the way of illustrations have survived of S & D coaches and wagons, but the locomotives were well photographed, largely in the 1860s and 1870s by that doyen of railway photographers, R. E. Bleasdale. He seems to have been given a free hand to photograph S & D and NER locomotives, and in recognition he appears to have presented the NER with a set of negatives of the company's engines, which remained at North Road Works until their closure in 1966.

In spite of the wholesale destruction of railway buildings in the last twenty years or so, it is still possible to find a number of S & D remains—if you know where to look! And, of course, there is (or was) quite a good selection of S & D items in the Railway Museum at York, and the BRB Archives, formerly at York but now in London under the control of the Public Record Office. It is a great pity that although the railway relics are being collected together in one large Museum at York, the railway records concerning the S & D and the NER have been transferred from York to London. This was a typical Government decision which fails to recognise what a magnificent collection could have been formed if the two had been combined at York. People would have come from all over the world to see the actual locomotives and the documents that went with them.

Perhaps the greatest tragedy, however, is British Railways' neglect of North Road station at Darlington. This is not the original station, which was opened in 1833, closed in 1842, and demolished in 1864, but the 1842 station. In spite of its disgraceful condition the station is still in use for passengers, although how British Railways expect anyone to use such a decrepit and dirty eyesore is beyond understanding. Fortunately there is a local scheme to take over the building and convert it into a railway museum, but money is the stumbling block. Perhaps there will be better news by the time this appears in print.

The same applies at Shildon, where Timothy Hackworth's cottage, and the sole remaining workshop from his Soho works, still stand but in a semi-derelict condition. Here again there is a plan to turn them into a local railway museum by 1975, to commemorate the first train which trundled past this very spot in 1825, with George Stephenson at the controls.

West of Shildon the earthworks of the line, particularly on the inclines, still bear witness to the manual labour put into the construction of the line 150 years ago, and it is still possible to locate some of the houses where the employees lived, distinguishable by the S & D house number plaque. At the actual terminus of the line at Witton Park extensive opencast coal workings have obliterated the site of the line, but from Low Etherley towards Shildon the course is easily visible, although not all of it is accessible due to many years of growth of bushes and trees on sections which have not persisted as footpaths.

At West Auckland, originally known as St Helen's, near the busy A688 road, it is still possible to locate the site of the first iron railway bridge in the world. Although it was replaced in 1901 it has fortunately been preserved at York. An original stone bridge still stands in a field near a minor road west of Shildon: a similar bridge nearby was demolished some years ago to improve the road. Shildon itself is worthy

11

of exploration: there is still plenty of S & D interest to see and the wagon works, busy turning out the latest type of wagons for British Railways, stand on the exact site of the repair shops originated by Timothy Hackworth all those years ago.

From Shildon to Darlington the present line runs on the original course and it is possible to travel over this section in the Bishop Auckland to Darlington pay-train service. After leaving North Road station trains now run into the former North Eastern station at Bank Top, where *Locomotion* and *Derwent* are on view, contrasting strongly with the 3300hp Deltic diesel-electric locomotives roaring past on the main line expresses.

From Darlington eastwards the original route is joined again at Oak Tree Junction, some four miles east of Darlington, and it is traversed as far as Eaglescliffe, passing on the way Allen's West station on the site of the old Yarm Branch End station. With the introduction of steam locomotives on the passenger trains in September 1833 the branch lost its regular service as the trains then stopped at the junction with the branch and the passengers had to walk to Yarm. From Eaglescliffe the old line was abandoned in 1853, when it moved to the other side of the main road, but the course can still be traced in the grounds of Preston Hall, now a museum.

From the present day Bowesfield Junction the 1825 line ran north eastwards to Stockton Quay, crossing the Stockton to Middlesbrough road (now A67) at St John's Crossing, where the first rail was laid in 1822. A railway building adjacent to the crossing, often referred to as the first railway booking office, has now been turned into a small railway museum. Beyond the crossing the line has been lifted.

Of course the section of line between Witton Park, through Shildon and Darlington, to Stockton, was not the full extent of the S & D—it was merely the first section opened. Between 1825 and 1863 the S & D continued to expand eastwards, westwards and northwards, usually under the name of some other company, for it was S & D practice to build lines in the guise of independent companies, so that if one line was unsuccessful it did not bring down the others. The Boards of these smaller companies were usually formed from the main S & D Board, plus a few influential local people, and every S & D line sponsored in this way was a success. All these companies became part of the S & D in the 1850s. Thus it is possible to trace the S & D to Saltburn in the east, Consett in the north, and Tebay and Penrith in the west, although S & D locomotives actually worked as far west as Cockermouth with trainloads of coke, traversing the jointly owned Cockermouth, Keswick & Penrith line from Penrith.

The last locomotives to S & D design were built in the 1870s when Bouch was still in charge of the Darlington Section engines. On his death in 1876 Fletcher designs began to infiltrate and some of the older S & D engines were transferred to other sections of the NER to end their days. A number of the famous long-boilered 0-6-0s went to Malton and Whitby to work the heavily graded and curved Whitby & Pickering line, and others worked on the isolated Rosedale line, which could only be reached via the massive rope worked Ingleby Incline. Only one S & D designed locomotive survived to be taken over by the LNER, No 1275, built by Dubs in 1874, which ended its days in February 1923 working from Malton shed. A couple of four-wheel coaches have been preserved but one, for long an exhibit on the platform at Stockton station, has now been removed.

Many stone blocks for the rails can be found, particularly from Darlington to Low Etherley. At one location, near Simpasture Junction, there are eighteen pairs of stone blocks on what was probably the original course of the line, and around Shildon such blocks can often be found in the grass and undergrowth where the line formerly ran.

In the Weatherhill area a number of boundary posts can still be seen, and many of the houses along the line carry a house number plaque—a square tile with a letter and one or two figures. The letter indicates the branch or area, and the figures the number of the house on the branch. The date on which this system was introduced has not been located, but from observation it appears that the letters ran from A in the east, across the North Riding and County Durham, to K in the north west. The plaques are not restricted to property adjacent to the line, but also appear on properties away from the line.

Numerous S & D items could be inspected in the Railway Museum at York— rails, chairs, signalling equipment, a chaldron wagon, a model of Belah viaduct, the tender from the locomotive *Etherley* (built by William Lister of Darlington in 1840), the Gaunless bridge from West Auckland, a small beam engine from Hackworth's Soho works, the winding engine from Weatherhill Incline, and a collection of small exhibits foo numerous to mention. It remains to be seen how many of these will be discarded when the exhibits are moved to the new museum, due to open on the exact anniversary of the opening of the S & D, 27 September 1975.

George Stephenson's part in the history of the S & D is well known, and has already been mentioned: he was brought into the S & D picture by a member of the Pease family, which was connected with the S & D from the very beginning, until 1863. Even then there was a Pease on the Board of the NER until that company succumbed in 1922, except for a period of eight months in 1905–6, between the resignation of Francis Richard Pease on 22 September 1905 and the appointment of Arthur Francis Pease on 25 May 1906. As Sir Arthur F. Pease, Bart, he was a director of the LNER until his death in November 1927. Can any other family in the British Isles show such a long and honourable connection with the railways of this country?

In 1891 Sir Joseph Pease and Mr J. A. Pease (and any friends travelling with them) were allowed to use the 6.19pm fish train from Newcastle to Darlington, and a suitable carriage had to be attached for their use: the train was then to be signalled as an express passenger.

In 1902, however, the Pease family lost some standing when the banking concern of J. & J. W. Pease suspended payment. At the time the NER had £230,754 9s 3d deposited with it; by raising money from friends the Pease family managed to repay some £105,000 to the NER, but the sum of £125,000 had to be written off. At the time Sir Joseph Pease, the principal partner in the bank, was chairman of the NER, having been elected to the Board when the S & D was taken over in 1863, and he immediately resigned.

The Kitching family of Darlington also had a long and involved connection with the S & D. In 1790 William Kitching established an ironmonger's shop in Darlington and six years later a small foundry was opened at the rear of the shop. In 1819

13

William died and the business was taken over by his two sons, William and Alfred. Both were interested in the proposed S & D and in 1824 they received their first order from the company—for nails to the value of £15 15s 0d. In September William Kitching was on the trial run made by *Locomotion* before the opening day, and as the railway business increased the brothers opened a new foundry in 1831, and in 1834, they commenced to build locomotives. In 1845 they built the locomotive *Derwent*, now preserved at Darlington, and in the same year William left the business leaving Alfred as the sole proprietor. However, in 1862 the premises were sold to the S & D for £12,100 and used as the carriage and wagon shops.

Alfred Kitching was a director of the Darlington & Barnard Castle Railway, the Frosterley & Stanhope, and the Stockton & Darlington. He was appointed to the Board of the NER in 1866 and remained a director until his death in 1882.

William Bouch was appointed locomotive foreman in 1840 upon the resignation of Timothy Hackworth, and he eventually became the engineer. He continued in charge of the locomotives and rolling stock after the North Eastern had taken over in 1863, turning out locomotives to old and tried designs. He played a large part in organising the celebrations held at Darlington in connection with the fiftieth anniversary of the S & D in 1875, but due to illness he was unable to be present at the events. He died at Weymouth on 19 January 1876.

It was William's brother Thomas Bouch, who was engineer of one of the major S & D projects of later days, the South Durham & Lancashire Union Railway, across the Pennines from West Auckland, through Barnard Castle and Kirkby Stephen, to Tebay. Thomas designed the famous viaducts on the route, the most notable being the Tees, Deepdale, and Belah bridges, opened in 1861. Ten years later he was responsible for the design of the ill-fated Tay Bridge, which collapsed with the loss of many lives as a train was passing over it in December 1879. The disgrace and worry occasioned by the collapse of the Tay Bridge brought about his death in the following year.

Other men who played an important part in the development of the S & D were Thomas MacNay, the secretary, and a director of a number of the subsidiary companies; John Dixon, engineer in chief; William Cudworth, engineer; Oswald Gilkes of the Shildon Works Company; George Stephenson, the traffic manager; and George Graham the outdoor manager. However, one man who never seems to have received due recognition is David Dale. He joined the S & D at an early age and by the time he had reached twenty-two he was secretary of the Middlesbrough & Guisborough Railway. After a wide experience in various positions on the S & D, where he proved invaluable in undertaking special duties placed upon him by the directors, he moved to the Consett Iron Co. and carried out a reorganisation of their affairs. He became a director of the NER in 1881 and died, as Sir David Dale, Bart, in 1906.

The hours of work at Shildon locomotive works were from 6.0am to 6.0pm, with thirty minutes for breakfast and an hour for dinner. On Saturdays the works closed at 3.0pm. No smoking was allowed on the premises (under penalty of a fine of 2s 6d); no workman was allowed to take a stranger or a dog on to the premises; no 'spirituous or malt liquor' was allowed, and the men were 'strictly cautioned against the use of profane and improper language, and the Company earnestly request them carefully

14

to abstain from a practice so degrading to themselves and offensive to others'.

The quality of the workmanship was important and 'it is intended that all work executed on these premises shall be the best of its kind that can be produced, in respect both of materials and workmanship; any workman, therefore, who shall use materials which appear to be improper, or unsound, or without having first consulted the foreman and having his express order to go on with the work, shall pay not only the value of the lost labour, but also that of the materials on which he lost his labour. Any workman executing unworkmanlike, defective, or inferior work and concealing its defects or trying to pass it, or have it passed, shall pay the full value of reinstating the same'.

In the 1850s, when the above rules were promulgated, the workmen were allowed to leave work at 4.0pm (instead of 6.0pm) each 27 September 'on the occasion of the Railway Birthday'.

At Darlington works, shortly after their opening in 1863, William Bouch issued a notice stating 'Workmen, Young Men, or Boys, employed in these works must understand that idleness or indolence will not be permitted within these walls'.

On the occasion of the Railway Jubilee in 1875 all S & D workmen with ten years and upwards service were allowed half a day off, with pay, to visit Darlington to see the exhibition of locomotives. For this they received a free pass, and 'a substantial plain dinner' at North Road works.

An early form of health service was introduced at Shildon works in 1846, when on payment of 2¼d per week a man could ensure medical attendance for himself, his wife, and family, although this did not include midwifery. In the following year, to encourage education of the children, the company paid part of the cost: where a child paid 3d per week the company paid 2d of it, and where a child paid 2d per week the company paid half. On 21 September 1849 the workmen were allowed to attend divine service during working hours as a thanksgiving for the cessation of the cholera epidemic, although nine years later they were being issued with disinfecting fluid, presumably because of another outbreak. The company also supplied gas and water to the inhabitants of Shildon.

Today the majority of Stockton & Darlington lines have been closed, most of them since the advent of British Railways, although some closed as long ago as the 1850s because of the replacement of rope-worked inclines by locomotive-worked lines on a new and more level course. However, much of the eastern end of the 1825 line is still in use between Stockton and Darlington, except for the diversion from Oak Tree Junction to Darlington, opened in 1887 to allow S & D line trains to use Bank Top station as well as North Road, and for the diversion at Eaglescliffe from one side of the main road to the other to allow the S & D and Leeds Northern to run side by side. Further east, through Thornaby (originally South Stockton), Middlesbrough, and Redcar, to Saltburn, later built sections are still in use and a journey from Saltburn to Bishop Auckland by ordinary passenger train involves travelling over the following lines:

LINE	ACT COMPANY	DATE	OPENED TO PASSENGERS	APPROX. DISTANCE (miles)
Saltburn to Warrenby Junction (Redcar)	S & D	23/7/1858	19/8/1861	6
Warrenby Junction to Dock Branch Junction (Middlesbrough)	M & R	21/7/1845	4/6/1846	6
Dock Branch Junction to Old Town Junction (Middlesbrough)*	M O	—	4/6/1846	¾
Old Town Junction to Stockton Goods Branch Junction (Bowesfield)	S & D	23/5/1828	27/12/1830	3¼
Stockton Goods Branch Junction to Stockton Cut	S & D	19/4/1821	27/9/1825	¼
Stockton Cut to Eaglescliffe South	S & D	13/7/1849	25/1/1853	2
Eaglescliffe South to Oak Tree Junction	S & D	19/4/1821	27/9/1825	5
Oak Tree Junction to Darlington South	NER	29/6/1883	1/7/1887	4
Darlington South to Albert Hill Junction (Croft branch)	S & D	23/5/1823	27/9/1829	1¼
Albert Hill Junction–Shildon	S & D	19/4/1821	27/9/1825	8
Shildon–South Church**	BA & W	15/7/1837	19/4/1842	2½
South Church to Bishop Auckland	BA & W	15/7/1837	8/11/1843	1

Notes: * Latterly known as Dock Hill Junction

** Shildon tunnel was owned by Joseph Pease, Thomas Meynell and Henry Stobart and it was built without Act of Parliament. Purchased by S & D 22/7/1847.

M & R   Middlesbrough & Redcar Railway

BA & W   Bishop Auckland & Weardale Railway

M O   Middlesbrough Owners.

AN

A C T

For making and maintaining a Railway or Tramroad from the River *Tees* at *Stockton*, to *Witton Park Colliery*, with several Branches therefrom, all in the County of *Durham*.

[Royal Assent, 19 *April* 1821.]

WHEREAS the making and maintaining of a Railway or Tramroad, for the passage of Waggons and other Carriages, from the River *Tees*, at or near *Stockton*, in the County of *Durham*, to *Witton Park Colliery*, in the Township of *Witton*, in the said County of *Durham*, with five collateral Branches from the said Railway or Tramroad; one of them commencing in the Township of *Egglescliffe*, and terminating at or near *Yarm Bridge*, in the said County of *Durham*; another of such collateral Branches commencing at or near *Lowson's Slack*, and terminating at or near *Northgate Bridge*, in the Township of *Darlington*, in the said County of *Durham*; another of such collateral Branches commencing at or near *Brussleton*, in the Township of *St. Helen's Auckland*, in the said County of *Durham*, and terminating at or near *Coundon* Turnpike Gate, in the Township of *Coundon*, in the said County of *Durham*; another of the said collateral Branches, commencing at or near *Norlees House*, in the Township of *West Auckland*, and terminating at or near *Evenwood Lane*, in the said County of *Durham*; and the other of such collateral Branches, commencing at or near the River *Tees*, and terminating at or near the South-west End of the Town of *Stockton-upon-Tees*, in the said County of *Durham*, will be

Preamble.

18.   A   of

PREAMBLE 1821 ACT *Page 17*

Although Parliamentary powers for the Stockton & Darlington Railway were sought in the 1818-9 session it was not until 19 April 1821 that the Royal Assent was given to the Bill to construct 'a railway or tramroad from the River Tees at Stockton to Witton Park Colliery, with five collateral branches'. The Act ran to sixty-eight pages and did not cover haulage by locomotives, authorising only the use of 'Men or Horses or otherwise'. Locomotives were not authorised until the 1823 Act.

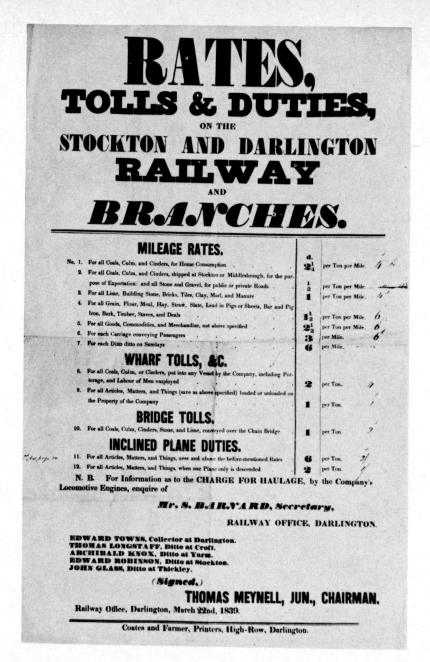

TOLLS *Page 18*
Notice giving Rates, Tolls and Duties on the Stockton & Darlington Railway in 1839.
The original notice is 11in × 8in.

TIMETABLE *Page 19 (top right)*
Half the timetable sheet giving the times of S & D trains in December 1855. Note that the fifty-four miles from Cold Rowley (at the extreme north west of the S & D system) to Redcar (at the extreme south east) took 4hr 10min.

CAUTIONS *(bottom right)*
Notice dated 1831 to ENGINE-MEN, WAGGON AND COACH DRIVERS ETC.

STOCKTON AND DARLINGTON RAILWAY COMPANY.

TIME TABLE FOR DECEMBER, 1855.

The Times shown in this Table are those before which the Trains will not depart from the various Stations; but the Company cannot guarantee any time, nor will they hold themselves responsible for delay. The granting Tickets to Passengers to places off the Company's line, is an arrangement made for the greater convenience of the public, but the Company do not hold themselves responsible for any delay, detention, or other loss or injury whatsoever arising off their Line, or from the acts or defaults of other parties.

Going East—from Stanhope, &c., to Redcar. | Going West—from Redcar to Stanhope, &c.

[Timetable grid — columns numbered 1 through 11 and Sundays, with station rows including Cold Rowley, Wackerley, Tow Law, Crook, Beechburn, Stanhope, Frosterley, Wolsingham, Witton-le-Wear, Junction, Bishop-Auckland, St. Helen's Auckland, Sheldon, Aycliffe and Heighington, Darlington, Middleton and Dinsdale, Yarm, Preston Junction for Leeds and Hartlepool, Stockton, Newport, Middlesbro', Ormesby, Nunthorpe, Pinchinghorpe, Guisbro', Cleveland Port, Eston, Lazenby, Redcar, Hartlepool and Seaton.]

TABLE SHOWING THE CONNEXION WITH TRAINS NORTH AND SOUTH.

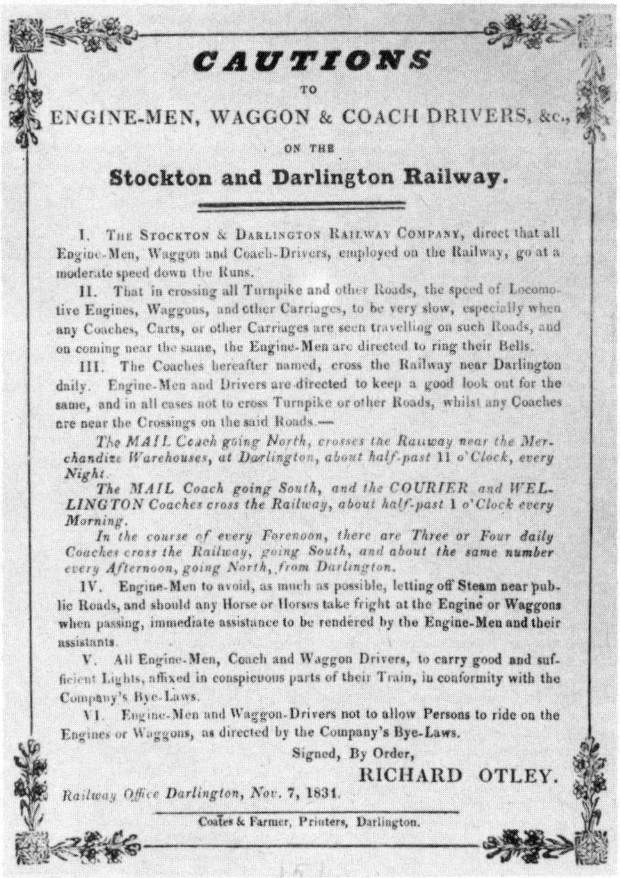

CAUTIONS
TO
ENGINE-MEN, WAGGON & COACH DRIVERS, &c.,
ON THE
Stockton and Darlington Railway.

I. THE STOCKTON & DARLINGTON RAILWAY COMPANY, direct that all Engine-Men, Waggon and Coach-Drivers, employed on the Railway, go at a moderate speed down the Runs.

II. That in crossing all Turnpike and other Roads, the speed of Locomotive Engines, Waggons, and other Carriages, to be very slow, especially when any Coaches, Carts, or other Carriages are seen travelling on such Roads, and on coming near the same, the Engine-Men are directed to ring their Bells.

III. The Coaches hereafter named, cross the Railway near Darlington daily. Engine-Men and Drivers are directed to keep a good look out for the same, and in all cases not to cross Turnpike or other Roads, whilst any Coaches are near the Crossings on the said Roads.—

The MAIL Coach going North, crosses the Railway near the Merchandize Warehouses, at Darlington, about half-past 11 o'Clock, every Night.

The MAIL Coach going South, and the COURIER and WELLINGTON Coaches cross the Railway, about half-past 1 o'Clock every Morning.

In the course of every Forenoon, there are Three or Four daily Coaches cross the Railway, going South, and about the same number every Afternoon, going North, from Darlington.

IV. Engine-Men to avoid, as much as possible, letting off Steam near public Roads, and should any Horse or Horses take fright at the Engine or Waggons when passing, immediate assistance to be rendered by the Engine-Men and their assistants.

V. All Engine-Men, Coach and Waggon Drivers, to carry good and sufficient Lights, affixed in conspicuous parts of their Train, in conformity with the Company's Bye-Laws.

VI. Engine-Men and Waggon-Drivers not to allow Persons to ride on the Engines or Waggons, as directed by the Company's Bye-Laws.

Signed, By Order,

RICHARD OTLEY.

Railway Office Darlington, Nov. 7, 1831.

Coates & Farmer, Printers, Darlington.

OPENING

OF THE

MIDDLESBRO' AND REDCAR RAILWAY.

THURSDAY, JUNE 4th, 1846.

ORDER OF THE ARRANGEMENTS FOR THE DAY.

THE TRAINS

Will leave Darlington	at 12	15 a.m.
Arrive at Fighting Cocks	at 12	25 "
" Yarm Branch	at 12	35 "
" Stockton	at 12	45 "
" Middlesbro'	at 1	0 p.m.
" Redcar	at 1	30 "

When the Directors will proceed to lay the Foundation Stone of the new Station House.

The Trains will take up Passengers at each of the places above named.

Dinner will be provided for the Gentlemen specially invited to meet the Directors on this occasion, at the Red Lion Hotel, Redcar, at 3 o'clock.

RETURNING.

Leaves Redcar	at 6	30 p.m.
Arrives at Middlesbro'	at 7	0 "
" Stockton	at 7	15 "
" Darlington	at 7	45 "

(Signed) by Order of the Board,

THOS. MAC NAY,

SECRETARY.

Railway Office, Darlington, May 28th, 1846.

N.B. The Public may be conveyed to Redcar, and return in connexion with these Trains, for ONE FARE THERE AND BACK, from any of the Stations on the Great North of England, Newcastle and Darlington, Stockton and Darlington, Bishop-Auckland and Weardale, and Derwent Junction Railways.

Tickets may be had by applying at the Coach Stations of the respective Companies, not later than Twelve o'clock, on Wednesday, the 3rd of June ; but no Tickets will be issued for the occasion, after that time.

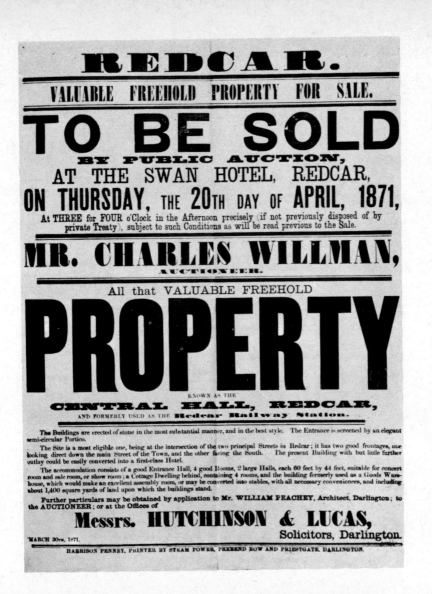

OPENING OF MIDDLESBROUGH & REDCAR RAILWAY *Page 20 (left)*
Notice issued for the opening of the Middlesbrough & Redcar Railway on 4 June 1846, when the inaugural train of a carriage and two wagons was worked by *Locomotion,* followed by Great North of England locomotive A, which had taken part in the Gauge Trials some months earlier. West of the new station at Middlesbrough the line (as far as the connection with the line to the original station) had been the property of the Middlesbrough Owners and had originally been built to serve the dock owned by the same consortium. The dock was opened in 1842 and taken over by the S & D in 1849

SALE OF OLD STATION AT REDCAR *Page 21 (top)*
When the time came to extend the line from Redcar to Saltburn it was impossible to project the line from the Redcar terminus and the new line had to branch off at Warrenby junction, about a mile outside the station, running on a more westerly course to pass behind the town. A new station was erected on this line and the old one was put up for sale by auction in 1870, and again in 1871. On neither occasion was it sold but the building was sold privately in 1873 and it remained in use, partly as a cinema, until it was demolished in the 1960s to make way for a modern shopping area development.

THE
Stockton and Darlington Railway Co.

ACT OF 1855

N°   £25 Share

This is to certify that

_____

the **PROPRIETOR** of the **SHARE**
NUMBERED _____, of the **Stockton and Darlington Railway Company.**
subject to the Rules, Regulations and Orders of the said Company.
Given under the **COMMON SEAL** of the said **COMPANY.** Dated the
Fifteenth day of August in the Year of our Lord One Thousand Eight Hundred
and Fifty Five.

Register Folio _____   *Tho⁵ Mac Nay*
                                                                Secretary

Wear Valley Railway.
"STOCKTON & DARLINGTON & WEAR VALLEY"
"SIX PER CENT GUARANTEED SHARES."

N°   £50 Share

This is to certify that

_____ is the **PROPRIETOR** of the **SHARE**
NUMBERED _____ of the **WEAR VALLEY RAILWAY COMPANY** subject to the
Rules, Regulations and Orders of the said Company.
Given under the **COMMON SEAL** of the said **COMPANY.**
the   day of   in the Year of our Lord One Thousand Eight Hundred
and

The form to be used in transfers is set out in the Company's Clauses Consolidation Act 1845 and a Memorial   Secretary
must be entered & a Certificate of the entry Endorsed on the Transfer by the Company's Secretary or Clerk.

THE MIDDLESBROUGH & GUISBROUGH Railway Company.

Act 15 Vict Cap 73.

N° 327

£25 SHARE

This is to certify that *Henry William Thomas of Pinchinthorpe near Guisbrough in the North Riding of the County of York Farmer*

is the Proprietor of the Share Numbered *Three hundred and twenty seven* in the **Middlesbrough and Guisbrough Railway Company**, subject to the Rules, Regulations and Orders of the said Company

Given under the **COMMON SEAL** of the said **COMPANY** the 1st day of October, in the Year of our Lord One Thousand Eight Hundred and Fifty Two

David Dale Secretary

STOCKTON & DARLINGTON RAILWAY £25 SHARE *Page 22 (top left)*
This shows the Skerne Bridge, made famous in Dobbin's painting of the opening day, with Darlington in the background. Prominent just to the right of centre is the Railway Mill in Northgate, owned by the Pease family. At the time Darlington was an important centre in the woollen industry;

WEAR VALLEY RAILWAY £50 SHARE *(bottom left)*
The rock cutting through which the train is passing represents the rich deposits of limestone found in the Wear valley, much of which was quarried by the S & D and transported to Middlesbrough for use in the blast furnaces there. Witton Castle is in the right background, with blast furnaces in the left background.

MIDDLESBROUGH & GUISBOROUGH RAILWAY £25 SHARE *Page 23 (top)*
Guisborough Priory and the town of Guisborough on the left and blast furnaces on the right, with the Eston Hills and Roseberry Topping in the background.

MIDDLESBRO' & REDCAR RAILWAY.
"Stockton · Darlington · Redcar."
"SIX PER CENT GUARANTEED SHARES."
ACT 8 & 9. VIC. CAP 127. SEC 36.

 N.º

 £50 SHARE

This is to certify that _____

_____

is the *Proprietor* of the *Share* Numbered ▬▬▬▬▬▬▬ *of the*
Middlesbro' and Redcar Railway Company, *subject to the Rules, Regulations and Orders of the said Company.*

Given under the **COMMON SEAL** of the said **COMPANY**
the 1st day of October, in the Year of our Lord One Thousand eight Hundred and forty Seven.—

_____ Secretary

The form to be used in Transfers is set out in the Company's Clauses Consolidation Acts 1845 and a Memorial must be Entered & a Certificate of the entry Endorsed on the Transfer by the Company's Secretary or Clerk.

MIDDLESBROUGH & REDCAR RAILWAY £50 SHARE *Page 24*
A train approaching Redcar, with Hunt Cliff (east of Saltburn and actually five miles beyond Redcar) on the right.

WORKING REGULATIONS *Page 25 (top right and left)*
This notice giving the REGULATIONS FOR WORKING THE SOUTH DURHAM LINE BETWEEN BARNARD CASTLE AND TEBAY was issued for the opening of the line in August 1861. The line was worked on the Staff and Ticket system and was divided into four sections.

CHANGE OF NAME OF STATION *(bottom right)*
The station at Howden, opened on 8 March 1869, was renamed Beechburn only a few weeks later, presumably to avoid confusion with Howden on the Hull to Selby line,and Howdon on the Tynemouth branch. Note that by this time the S & D had become the Darlington Section of the North Eastern Railway.

Stockton & Darlington Railway Company.

REGULATIONS FOR WORKING THE SOUTH DURHAM LINE BETWEEN BARNARD CASTLE AND TEBAY.

GENERAL INSTRUCTIONS.

The Line is to be worked by what is designated the "Train Staff" mode of working.

Either a Train Staff or a Train Ticket is to be carried with each Engine or Train to and fro, and no Engine or Train is to be allowed to start without one of these.

The Line will be divided into 4 Sections, and 4 Staffs will be employed thereon,—

One between Barnard Castle and Bowes	with Yellow Staff.
" "	Bowes and Summit	"	Blue	"
" "	Summit and Kirkby Stephen	"	White	"
" "	Kirkby Stephen and Tebay	"	Red	"

No Engine or Train is to be permitted to leave any of the above Stations unless a Staff is at the Station.

If no 2nd Engine or Train is intended to follow, the Staff is to be given to the Guard or the person in charge.

If another Engine or Train is intended to follow, before the Staff can be returned, a Train Ticket stating "Staff following" will be given to the person in charge of the preceding Train, the Staff itself being given to the person in charge of the last Train, after which no Engine or Train can leave the Station under any circumstances whatever, until the Staff is returned.

The Train Tickets are to be kept in charge of competent persons at Barnard Castle, Bowes, Summit, Kirkby Stephen and Tebay.

The Train Tickets and the Ticket Boxes are to be the same Colour as the Staff to which they apply.

Any Guard or Engineman, taking a Staff or Ticket beyond the portion of Line to which it belongs, or leaving a Station without the Staff, or without a Ticket, as heretofore explained, will render himself liable to dismissal, although no accident may ...

No Engineman is to start from any of the Stations until the Guard connected with his Train has shewn him the Train Staff or Ticket.

2

The usual Special Train Signals are to be used for the guidance of the Gate-keepers and Platelayers. A Red Board or Flag by day, or an additional lighted Red Tail Lamp placed on the Train or Engine by night, denotes that another Train or Engine is following.

Ballast Trains are to be treated in every respect like Traffic Trains as regards the Staff and Ticket arrangements.

In the event of an Engine or Train breaking down between two Stations, the Fireman is to take the Train Staff to the Station in the direction whence assistance may be expected, that the Staff may be at the Station on the arrival of an Engine. Should the Engine that fails be in possession of a Train Ticket, instead of the Staff, assistance can only come from the Station at which the Train Staff has been left.

The Fireman must in such a case procure a "Red Flag" by day or "hand Signal Lamp" by night and return to the nearest Telegraph Station, or until he meets an Engine or Train with the Train Staff, taking care to place an explosive signal on the rails at a distance of 400 yards from the disabled Train, and two such signals when at a distance of 800 yards.

All parties concerned in the carrying out of these Regulations are expected not only to strictly adhere to them, but also, to report to the Superintendent of Police (Mr. R. Brown, Railway Station, Darlington,) any infringement they may observe by others.

These Regulations are issued by the Stockton & Darlington Board, for circulation amongst their Agents and Workmen engaged in working the Traffic between Barnard Castle and Tebay.

Signed,

THOS. MAC NAY.

Railway Offce,
Darlington, August, 1861.

N.B.—Until further Notice, Barras Station shall not be used as a Passenger Station, nor shall there be 2 Engines in Steam at one and the same time, between Barnard Castle and Lartington, nor between Newbiggen and Gaisgill.

400—4-69.

NORTH EASTERN RAILWAY.
DARLINGTON SECTION.
NOTICE.
HOWDEN STATION.

The Passenger Station opened at Howden on March 8th, 1869, will henceforth be called and known by the name of

BEECHBURN STATION.

Darlington, *April 16th*, 1869.

GEORGE STEPHENSON
Page 26

George Stephenson was born in 1781 in a cottage known as Street House, at the side of the Wylam Wagonway, on the north bank of the Tyne west of Newcastle. The wagonway formation was later used for the Scotswood, Newburn & Wylam Railway, opened in 1876, but although the latter line has been closed and lifted the cottage is still there and occupied, under the control of the National Trust. Stephenson moved to Killingworth in 1804 and it was there that he carried out some of his most important work on the steam locomotive. The line from the pits at Killingworth to the staiths on the River Tyne ran behind the cottage but it has now been lifted. Here again the cottage is still occupied. Over the door is a sundial George made with his son Robert.

TIMOTHY HACKWORTH
Page 27

Timothy Hackworth was appointed locomotive foreman of the S & D in May 1825 — some four months before the first locomotive was delivered — but Hackworth had already had experience of locomotives at collieries on Tyneside and at the works of Stephenson & Co. Hackworth lived in Soho Cottage, on the south eastern outskirts of New Shildon, and here he established a locomotive building works. Although he continued to look after S & D locomotives this was as a contractor and not as an employee, and thus he was able to set up his own works, where he built locomotives for Russia and Nova Scotia, as well as for English railways.

A statue in his memory was unveiled as late as 1925, seventy-five years after his death.

TIMOTHY HACKWORTH
1786 — 1850

JOSEPH PEASE *Page 28*

The statue of Joseph Pease, the first treasurer of the S & D, was unveiled on the High Row at Darlington on 27 September 1875 as part of the celebrations to commemorate the fiftieth anniversary of the Stockton & Darlington Railway. Great credit is usually given to Edward Pease, but most of the work in connection with the railway was performed by his sons, Joseph and Henry. The statue, in polished Peterhead granite, is by G. A. Lawson: it does not now stand in its original position as it was moved slightly some years ago to facilitate road improvements at this busy corner of Darlington.

EDWARD PEASE

The 2-4-0 locomotive named after Edward Pease was built by Robert Stephenson & Co. in August 1856. It honoured the senior member of the Pease family who did so much towards the founding and opening of the Stockton & Darlington Railway. At the time the engine was built Edward Pease was in his 90th year and he died two years later.

SHILDON *Page 29*
The Masons' Arms level crossing at Shildon has become famous because it was here that *Locomotion* was attached to the first train on 27 September 1825, after the wagons had been lowered down Brusselton south incline, and a plaque giving this information is affixed nearby. The original hostelry was used as the railway booking office in the 1830s and a public house of the same name still stands adjacent to the crossing, which is across the road from Darlington to Bishop Auckland (A 6072) in the centre of Shildon.

FROM SHILDON. NEAR THIS SITE.
THE STOCKTON AND DARLINGTON
RAILWAY COMPANY. ON THE
27TH. SEPTEMBER. 1825.
RAN THE FIRST PASSENGER TRAIN
DRAWN BY A STEAM ENGINE.

Notice at Masons' Arms level crossing at Shildon.

29

DARLINGTON *Page 30 (top and bottom left)*
The present North Road station was opened in 1842 and during its life has undergone
a number of changes internally, although the exterior has altered little. However, the
original design, still held in the engineer's office at York, shows a much more elaborate
design than was actually built. The station is still used by trains between Darlington and
Bishop Auckland but is in no state to attract passengers to this subsidised service!
The first coach station at Darlington was part of the merchandise warehouse on the
east side of North Road. In 1833 the upper floor was converted to a dwelling house and
shop and let to Mary Simpson at £25 a year on condition that she kept the coach office
clean and 'afforded every necessary accommodation to passengers!' The building was
demolished in 1864.

Page 31 (top)
Adjacent to the 1842 passenger station at North Road a solidly built goods station was
built, surmounted by a square clock tower. The building has latterly been used by the
road motor engineer for vehicle repairs.

Page 32 (top left)
North Road station west end c 1908 with a Class 901 2-4-0 on a Kirkby Stephen train.

(bottom left)
North Road station 1957. Work has now started on converting the station into a railway museum.

Page 33 (top)
Skerne Bridge, Darlington, the subject of the famous Dobbin painting.

FIGHTING COCKS *Page 34 (top left)*
The early horse drawn coaches halted at the point where the line crossed the road from Middleton St George to Sadberge,and what better place for the passengers to wait than in the warmth of the nearby hostelry, The Fighting Cocks? Consequently when a cottage for the accommodation of passengers and parcels was authorised in 1830 the stopping place was called Fighting Cocks, developing into the station of that name. The level crossing still retains the name, even though the passenger service was withdrawn in 1887 and the goods service in 1964: however, the line is still open to allow goods trains to serve works on the east side of Darlington. Of interest is the unusual waiting room on the northern platform, unlike any other surviving S & D building.

ST JOHN'S CROSSING *(bottom left)*
The first rails were laid at St John's Crossing by the chairman, Thomas Meynell, on 23 May 1822, after a procession from Stockton Town Hall. The line to the Quay was closed in 1967 and the level crossing gates were removed on 24 April 1969 and replaced by a fence, thus effectively bringing to an end the life of a line which had been born in the very early days of the S & D. However, the line from Bowesfield Junction to Stockton Goods station nearby, and to the coal depots behind the house, both on the south side of the road, is still in use.

BOWESFIELD JUNCTION *Page 35 (top)*
Bowesfield Junction in 1959 looking towards Thornaby and Middlesbrough. It was at this point that the Middelsbrough branch of 1830 diverged from the 1825 line to Stockton. The curve coming in on the left is the connection to the Leeds Northern line at Hartburn Junction.

35

ST JOHNS' CROSSING *Page 36*

The early horse-drawn coaches on the S & D terminated at Stockton on the Quay, not far behind the houses and shops which lined the large Market Place. At a later date—probably about the time locomotive haulage was introduced on the coach trains in 1833 — a passenger terminus was established at St John's Crossing. A house on the east side of the line was used as a booking office, and for the guidance of train crews and passengers a clock was fitted into the west wall of the building; the bricked up hole where it once ticked away the hours can still be seen. A plaque stating that this was where the first railway passenger was booked was unveiled by the Duke of York as part of the 1925 Centenary celebrations. This building now houses a small railway museum.

BRUSSELTON *Page 37 (top right)*

To reach its objective at Witton Park the original line of the S & D had to surmount two ridges of land north west of Shildon. The first of these was at Brusselton, less than a mile west of Masons' Arms level crossing, worked by a stationary engine and a rope 825yd long. According to an old sketch the winding drums were mounted over the tracks and the outline of the engine house can still be seen in the wall of a building on the south side of the trackbed. A number of cottages for S & D workmen were built at the incline top and until well into LNER days these houses were supplied with coal by a pilot engine working a wagon or two up the incline. On the other side of the ridge the line descended an incline 1,850yd long, followed by a horse-worked stretch to the foot of Etherley south incline, just north of the River Gaunless bridge.

ETHERLEY INCLINE TOP *(bottom right)*

Etherley south incline was self-acting; that is, the descending loaded wagons hauled up the empty wagons by means of a rope round a pulley at the top, without the aid of a winding engine. However, the final incline, Etherley north, was engine worked over its 1,100yd and an engine house stood at the summit, some 500yd south of the village of Low Etherley. The engine house fell into disuse in 1858 and has since disappeared as use has been found for the stones with which it was built. However, the enginemen's cottages, now converted into one house, still stand, with the house number plaque H5.

WEST AUCKLAND *Page 38*

At the northern end of the level section between the foot of Brusselton north and Etherley south inclines the line was carried across the River Gaunless on a cast and wrought iron bridge — the world's first on a railway. The bridge was designed by George Stephenson and completed in 1823 with three spans, but floods in the following year caused damage to the structure and a fourth span was added. Although the line fell into disuse after the opening of the Tunnel branch in 1856 the bridge remained in place until 1900, when it was replaced by a bridge suitable for locomotives, in connection with the re-opening of the line as far as Brusselton Colliery siding, on 20 May 1901. Fortunately the original bridge was preserved by the NER and for the last forty years it has been in York Museum. The second bridge has also gone now, but the site is little changed from what it was like in 1825.

HAGGERLEASES BRANCH
Page 39

The northern terminus for passengers was at St Helen's Auckland (often referred to as St Helen's and, from April 1878, renamed West Auckland) at the foot of Etherley south incline, and adjacent to the Bishop Auckland–Barnard Castle turnpike. To serve coal workings to the west, up the Gaunless valley, the Haggerleases branch was opened from St Helen's in 1830. It was not until September 1856 that locomotives were used on the branch: until then the coal wagons had been drawn by horses. A sparse passenger service was introduced on the branch in October 1858. Almost at the extremity of the branch is a stone skew bridge which, in spite of predictions that it would not stand, is still there today.

The NER zero post at Spring Gardens Junction treats the Haggerleases line as the branch, but the line was there thirty-three years before the South Durham route to Barnard Castle was opened from this junction.

BLACK BOY BRANCH *Page 40 (top left)*
Progress northwards from Shildon was also blocked by a ridge of high land, but as there were collieries to serve north of this ridge the Black Boy branch was constructed up one side and down the other. For the first few weeks after its opening in July 1828 the line was worked by horses, but for many years afterwards it was operated by a winding engine at the summit. However, the importance of the line decreased with the boring of a tunnel through the ridge. Much of the southern incline is now a wide well-kept footpath, but the site of the northern incline is a rough track, little different from when the rails were lifted some forty years ago. At one time both inclines were available as a through route for locomotive hauled trains in the event of a blockage by derailment or collision in the tunnel.

SHILDON *(bottom left)*
The Black Boy branch diverged from the S & D 1825 line at the point where Timothy Hackworth erected his Soho works, and from this spot a privately owned branch, known as the Surtees Railway, went off to serve Coppy Crooks colliery, north west of Shildon. Over this branch, and on to Darlington, a horse-drawn coach service was provided by Dan Adamson, landlord of the Grey Horse inn (still there as the Surtees Arms) and to shelter his coach from the weather he built a coach shed on the opposite side of the road to the inn. The line subsequently served Shildon Lodge colliery and remained in use until about 1930. Road improvements have removed all traces of the line but the coach shed is still there. Nearer Soho the course of the line can be plainly seen.

SHILDON TUNNEL *Page 41 (top)*
Shildon tunnel, 1,217yd long, was constructed privately and sold to the S & D in 1847 for £223,450. It was opened in 1842 and provided a much improved route from Shildon to the north without the need to traverse the Black Boy inclines. At one time traffic was so heavy that trains had to queue to get through the tunnel and a system of priorities had to be introduced. At that time there were two tracks but because of limited clearance this has been reduced to one. Now all that passes through the tunnel is the pay-train service between Darlington and Bishop Auckland, the cement traffic from Eastgate, rubbish for Etherley Tip, and some freight for Bishop Auckland. Since the closure of the Bishop Auckland to Durham route there is no through line to the north.

SOUTH CHURCH *Page 42 (top left)*

When Shildon tunnel was opened the track to the north reached only as far as South Church, about a mile beyond the tunnel and adjacent to the road to Durham. Thus from April 1842 until November 1843 South Church was the northern terminus of the line and a horse bus service was provided to connect with the Durham Junction trains at Rainton Meadows, some six miles north east of Durham. On 8 November 1843 the line was extended to Bishop Auckland and Crook, and South Church became redundant, although the station buildings remained in use as a dwelling house until quite recently.

(bottom left)

Shildon station was built at the point where the line through Shildon tunnel (right) branched off the 1825 line (left). The station is still open as an unstaffed halt, and the 1825 line is still open to the foot of Brusselton incline to serve Shildon wagon works.

BISHOP AUCKLAND *Page 43 (top)*

Bishop Auckland was reached in November 1843 when the South Church–Crook section was opened: at first facilities provided were very sparse, but with the coming of the NER from Leamside and Durham in 1857 Bishop Auckland increased in size and importance, becoming a joint S & D/NER station in 1857 with the formation of a Joint Station Committee. The two S & D representatives appointed to the Committee were Col Stobart and Henry Pease, and for the NER Mr Plews and Mr Wharton.

BISHOP AUCKLAND *Page 44*

The S & D section of the station at Bishop Auckland consisted of a single platform handling passenger traffic in both directions and this remains in use today for the Darlington service. With the take-over of the S & D by the NER in 1863 the need for a Joint Committee disappeared. In its final form the station had a triangular layout, with platforms inside the triangle on three sides, but outside the triangle on only one. The addition of new awnings, entrances and platforms obliterated parts of the original station but these have been revealed again with the demolition that took place in the 1960s.

CROOK *Page 45 (top right)*

The original station at Crook was a terminus opened in November 1843 when the line was extended from South Church. At a later date the S & D agreed to co-operate with the Derwent Iron Co. in building a line from Crook to Waskerley and subsequently a new station was built on the extension line about half mile north of the original terminus. The second station, closed to passenger traffic in March 1965, has since been demolished, but the original station buildings were converted into a row of cottages and as such still stand, although not recognisable as a one time station. However, the cottage at the north end of the block still retains traces of a ticket window but on an *inside* wall.

CROOK GOODS STATION *(bottom right)*

The goods shed at Crook remained on the site adjacent to the original passenger station after the opening of the second Crook station. This was an interesting old building, demolished in the 1960s. The whole area on the east side of the original station has been grassed over and it is difficult to tell that this spot was once a hive of railway industry. However, the row of cottages converted from the old station still carries a nameplate lettered GOODS STATION.

ELDON LANE LIMEKILNS *Page 46*
The S & D built large kilns for burning the lime quarried in Weardale. The largest were at Bishopley, on a quarry branch diverging from the line to Frosterley, and another set was established at Eldon Lane, near the north end of Shildon tunnel. The latter came into operation in December 1845 but have long been derelict, although still easily recognisable when photographed in 1967.

BISHOPLEY BRANCH *Page 47 (top right)*
Bishopley quarry and kilns were owned by the S & D but were usually worked by a contractor, who took over the equipment at valuation and continued to work the quarry and burn the lime. The quarry and kilns were subsequently sold but although the quarry was worked out in the 1920s the kilns continue to operate with limestone from other large quarries in the area, conveyed to Bishopley by road. The Bishopley branch itself closed in 1928, but it is still possible to explore its course near White Kirkley.

TOW LAW *(bottom right)*
When the Stanhope & Tyne Railroad found itself in financial difficulties in 1840 the outlook was bleak for the Derwent Iron Co., cut off from its supply of limestone from Stanhope, and from its only rail outlet. An alternative route to the south to join up with the Bishop Auckland & Weardale line at Crook was proposed, and although the Iron Co. intended to build the line themselves it was actually built by the S & D under the title of the Weardale Extension Railway. Between Crook and Tow Law the line had to climb 500ft up what became known as Sunnyside incline, although in 1867 it was replaced by a new line which could be worked by locomotives. Passenger services north of Tow Law were withdrawn on 1 May 1939, and Tow Law itself lost its train service when the trains were cut back to Crook in June 1956. Tow Law station has now disappeared and the site is covered with houses.

WASKERLEY ENGINE SHED
Page 48

The opening of the Stanhope & Tyne from Stanhope Kilns to South Shields in 1834 brought a touch of civilisation to the wild moors of north west Durham, and the arrival of the Weardale Extension Railway from Crook and Tow Law in 1845 brought into being a through (but roundabout) route from the Tees to the Tyne. The line from the south joined the former S & T line at Waskerley and it was there, on the very top of the moors, that the S & D decided to build a locomotive shed, wagon repair shop, and sidings, together with cottages for the employees, a church to minister to their spiritual needs, and a school for their children, with the schoolmaster paid for by the railway company. For many years this almost self-sufficient community thrived in its isolation, but the decrease in traffic led to the closure of the engine shed in 1940 and now the village is almost deserted, with the line closed and lifted.

Early pattern water column fed from a small reservoir on the moors near Parkhead, on the line from Waskerley to Weatherhill incline top.

WASKERLEY 1963 *Page 49*
For many years the engines stationed at Waskerley were the Bouch 0-6-0s with all the wheels in front of the firebox, although previously the line had been the last haunt of the double-tender engines favoured by Hackworth and perpetuated by Bouch. In LNER days the allocation usually consisted of former NER 0-6-2T engines for the goods and mineral traffic, with a 2-4-0, 4-4-0, or 0-6-0 for the twice daily passenger train between Blackhill and Darlington. Engines known to have worked this train include 23 and 678 of Class D23, 777 of Class D22, 4386 of Class D3, and 807 of Class J21, The line had its moments of glory, perhaps the most notable being in September 1963 when, in the course of the five-day North Eastern Region tour organised by the SLS and RCTS, Waskerley was visited by a six-coach train (including buffet-car) worked by spotless K1 2-6-0 62027.

WEATHERHILL INCLINE *Page 50 (top left)*
Weatherhill was at the summit of two rope-worked inclines serving the limestone quarries on the northern slopes of the Wear valley. Originally opened by the Stanhope & Tyne in 1834, the line was taken over by the Stockton & Darlington and continued in use from Weatherhill to Consett until 1968. Latterly a triple expansion engine was used for operating the winding drum at Weatherhill: previously a beam engine was used and when it was replaced in 1916 it was preserved by the NER and it eventually found a home in the Railway Museum at York. The ruins of the old beam engine house remained in existence for many years, standing starkly against the sky-line, until demolished in the 1960s (right). The new engine house is on the extreme left.

HOG HILL TUNNEL *(bottom left)*
Limestone from the quarries above Stanhope was supplied to the Derwent (later Consett) Iron Co. and also to the large Stanhope & Tyne kilns at East Castles (near Annfield Plain). However, kilns adjacent to the quarries were also used and a network of lines served both quarries and kilns, with one of the buildings retaining a Stockton & Darlington house number plaque. With better and more convenient sources of limestone the workings at Stanhope have been allowed to run down. Access to the kilns was through Hog Hill tunnel.

HOWNES GILL VIADUCT *Page 51 (top)*
Hownes Gill viaduct still remains but it no longer carries a railway. It was built in 1858 to replace two inclined planes, one down each side of the ravine. Until 1939 the viaduct carried a passenger service between Darlington and Blackhill: when that ceased all that was left was freight and sand traffic from Burnhill, Blanchland (originally Parkhead) and Weatherhill. The line closed completely in April 1968. The bridge, 730ft long and 150ft maximum height, cost £15,756 and 2,655,000 bricks were used in its construction.

SPRING GARDENS JUNCTION *Page 52*

Spring Gardens Junction was the point where the South Durham & Lancashire Union Railway to Barnard Castle (opened in 1863) diverged from the S & D Haggerleases branch of 1830. A large amount of westbound coke traffic and eastbound ore traffic passed between Bishop Auckland and the west via Spring Gardens Junction, and in the summer months Newcastle–Blackpool passenger trains used the line. During the winter months the line was served by Sunderland–Durham–Bishop Auckland–Barnard Castle–Middleton in Teesdale trains, but passenger traffic between Bishop Auckland and Barnard Castle ceased in June 1962, At one time the Haggerleases branch was a hive of industry, serving numerous coal mines in the Gaunless valley, but as these pits closed down there was only Randolph colliery coke traffic remaining, and when this ceased in August 1968 the Haggerleases branch was finished. The coke ovens continue to operate but the traffic is now carried by road transport.

LANDS VIADUCT *Page 53 (top right)*

The Haggerleases branch kept to the banks of the River Gaunless as it ran along the floor of the valley, whereas the South Durham & Lancashire Union, striking off at Spring Gardens Junction, climbed to surmount Cockfield Fell. In $2\frac{1}{2}$ miles the latter had gained sufficient height to cross the valley (and the Haggerleases branch) on a large viaduct, seen here in its original (1863) condition. The girders were renewed in 1905 when various sections of the Barnard Castle line were being doubled. The girders were salvaged after the line closed in 1962 but the piers remain.

BELAH VIADUCT *(bottom right)*

The South Durham & Lancashire Union Railway required some magnificent viaducts in some magnificent settings, particularly between Barnard Castle and Kirkby Stephen. Belah viaduct, in its bleak and wild moorland setting, was a fine sight, especially with an eastbound train passing slowly across against the gradient. Belah was 1,040ft long, with a maximum height of 196ft, but it has been demolished since the line closed on 20 January 1962. Because of weight restrictions on the viaducts only the lighter classes of engines were allowed on the line, although surprisingly, the restrictions were relaxed in the 1950s and heavier engines began to appear.

ENGINE SHED AT COCKERMOUTH *Page 54*

When the line over the Pennines was under discussion there were two schools of thought, one wanting the proposed line to connect with the Lancaster & Carlisle Railway at Penrith, and the other at Tebay. When Tebay was chosen as the western terminus of the South Durham line a new company was quickly formed to build a line from Kirkby Stephen to Penrith under the title of the Eden Valley Railway. It was opened from Kirkby Stephen to Clifton, south of Penrith, in 1862, but a new connection with the west coast main line, facing in the opposite direction, was put in nearer Penrith at what later became Eden Valley Junction, in 1863. Stockton & Darlington engines worked over the Cockermouth, Keswick & Penrith joint line as far as Cockermouth, where an engine shed — still standing — was erected for their use.

SUSPENSION BRIDGE *Page 55 (top right)*

On the Middlesbrough Extension of the S & D, opened on 27 December 1830, the River Tees was crossed on a suspension bridge designed by Capt S. Brown, who confidently predicted that it would be suitable for rail traffic. His forecast proved to be wrong and although wagons were hauled across the bridge they could only be handled four at a time, and then connected by a chain which spaced them 27ft apart. The suspension bridge was replaced in 1841 by a cast iron bridge with three spans of 89ft, and two shore spans of 31ft. This bridge was replaced in 1907 using the original piers, which are still in use today.

MIDDLESBROUGH DOCK *(bottom right)*

Middlesbrough Dock was built by a consortium known as the Middlesbrough Owners, in which the Pease family played a large part, and it was opened on 12 May 1842. It could accommodate 150 ships of the time and the main trade was in coal. The dock was taken over by the S & D in 1849 but the large network of lines and sidings remained in the hands of the Middlesbrough Owners until 1864. Work on enlarging the dock commenced in 1869 and this was completed in 1874. In the last twenty years further large scale development has taken place on the Tees but this has been further downstream on reclaimed land, leaving the dock unaffected except for a decrease in traffic.

DEEPDALE VIADUCT *Page 56*
Deepdale viaduct, on the eastern side of the Pennines, has also been demolished. This bridge was in a softer setting than Belah and could best be appreciated when there were no leaves on the trees. Its height was 161ft and its total length was 740ft with eleven iron spans each of 60ft. It cost £20,687.

MIDDLESBROUGH SHED *Page 58*
Middlesbrough shed c 1900 with two North Eastern 0-6-0s (left) and two Stockton
& Darlington 0-6-0s (right).

REDCAR
The original station at Redcar was at the terminus of the line from Middlesbrough
opened in 1846, but when an extension to Saltburn was authorised in 1858 it was found
impractical to continue the existing line. Thus the extension had to leave the old line at
Warrenby and run on a more westerly course, with a new station. This was of the typical
S & D single platform type to handle traffic in both directions. An additional platform
was constructed in 1935 for Saltburn–Middlesbrough trains but the station returned to
its original single-platform style in 1970.

ZETLAND HOTEL, SALTBURN *Page 59*
Saltburn was reached on 18 August 1861 and the S & D sponsored the Saltburn Improvement Company, formed to build houses to attract new residents — and thus more passengers for the line. An additional attraction was the Zetland Hotel, opened in July 1863 and still under railway control. The hotel was served by an extension of one of the platforms at Saltburn station and this was used for fuel and laundry supplies: it was removed in January 1970.

Silver dish used at the Zetland Hotel, Saltburn.

SHILDON *Page 60 (top left)*
Numerous photographs of Stockton & Darlington locomotives show the engine sheds at Shildon in the background, but no photograph of the buildings themselves is known. In this view of *Wilberforce*, for instance, only a small portion of one of the sheds can be seen. Just behind the photographer were the locomotive works but, unfortunately, he didn't photograph those either!

SHILDON *(bottom left)*
To house the large number of locomotives working from Shildon three circular sheds were erected between 1854 and 1865, but they were renewed on the same site between 1886 and 1892. However, instead of having three separate buildings the new shed incorporated three turntables in line under one roof. The running shed declined in importance in the 1930s with the contraction of the West Durham coal industry and it was closed on 8 July 1935. In the following year authority was given to include the former shed building in the wagon works complex and the necessary alterations were completed in 1938. This building, on the north side of the line to Brusselton, still remains in use. Between 1915 and 1935 the shed housed the ten electric locomotives built for working the mineral trains to Newport (near Middlesbrough).

Page 61 (top)
Electric train leaving Shildon on 1 July 1915.

61

SOHO WORKS *Page 62 (top left)*
In this view of Timothy Hackworth's Soho works the foundry is on the left (with tall chimney); the centre section was the machine shop; and the right-hand section housed the boilersmiths and blacksmiths. The small chimney stack seen on the extreme right is the one on the left of the building in the illustration below. The buildings were demolished in 1946.

SOHO WORKS *(bottom left)*
Timothy Hackworth was appointed locomotive superintendent of the S & D in May 1825 (before the line actually opened) and he was responsible for keeping running the miscellaneous collection of engines acquired by the company in its formative years. In 1833 the S & D introduced a system whereby the locomotives were operated and maintained by contractors. Hackworth was the main contractor, maintaining the S & D locomotives at Shildon works, but as he was no longer an employee of the company he decided to set up his own locomotive building establishment at Soho, some half mile away from the S & D works and adjacent to Shildon station. In 1840 he decided to sever his connection with the S & D and to devote all his time to his own works, and this he did until his death in 1850 at the age of 63.

Page 63 (top)
The west end of Hackworth's erecting shop at Shildon.

SOHO WORKS PAINT SHOP *Page 64 (top)*

In 1855 Soho works were purchased by the S & D and used as an extension to Shildon works until February 1883, when the men at Soho were moved to the main works, then beginning to develop as a wagon building centre. Some of the Soho works buildings were subsequently used as a gasworks, and all but one were demolished in 1946. The remaining building, shown as a pattern store in Robert Young's book on Timothy Hackworth, was used by the S & D as a locomotive paint shop, and there are in existence photographs showing engines receiving their finishing touches outside the shop, before being returned to traffic. In NER and LNER days the same building was used as a band room, and as a gymnasium, but it is now empty and suffering from the attention of the local vandals. A recent examination revealed that the rails and inspection pits are still under the floor, and in what was the boiler house there are some lengths of fish-bellied rail, complete with chairs.

LOCOMOTIVE COAL STAGE *Page 64 (bottom left)*
To supply the locomotives with coal a large stone coal stage was erected at Shildon in 1847, in the V of the junction between the original line of 1825 and the line through Shildon tunnel. Coal was dropped through the bottom doors of the wagons into large hoppers built into the stage, and then fed from the hoppers into the engine tenders as required. The stage was half mile from the shed, which meant using Masons' Arms level crossing, and engines travelling between the shed and the stage had to carry a special green light at night. The coal stage remained in use until the shed closed in July 1935 and still stands after almost forty years of disuse.

BOILER EXPLOSION *Page 65*
The boiler of 0-6-0 590 exploded on 17 July 1888, again at Simpasture, and although not a true S & D engine it had been built at Darlington in 1879. Up to the time of the explosion it had run 220,705 miles, during which time it had been in the charge of the driver involved in the explosion. Fortunately neither driver nor fireman were killed and after the explosion they jumped on to the track while the train was still moving. However, it was travelling only slowly and by dropping wagon brakes as the train passed them they managed to bring it to a standstill. The engine was scrapped but a replacement engine was built, although on entering traffic it was allocated the number 17, and 590 was allocated to a new crane tank engine.

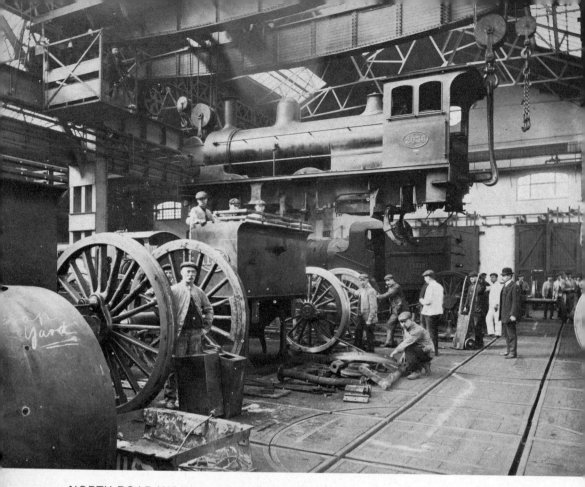

NORTH ROAD WORKS, DARLINGTON *Page 66*
In 1854 John Dixon suggested that thought should be given to the future location of
the S & D engine works. Shildon was not ideally suitable because of its position towards
the northern end of the line, and after three years of discussion it was decided to build
the new works at Darlington: originally it was intended that only the passenger engines
and those used on the line to Tebay (then only in the planning stage) should be maintained at Darlington, leaving the goods and mineral engines to be maintained at Shildon,
where most of them were stationed. The new works, facing on to North Road, were
opened on 1 January 1863 and eventually became responsible for the maintenance
of all the locomotives in the North Eastern Area of the LNER and the North Eastern
Region of BR. In addition 2,775 steam and diesel locomotives were built at Darlington
between 1864 and 1964.

NORTH ROAD WORKS, DARLINGTON *Page 67 (top right)*
The works were extended at various times, the most notable addition being the large
erecting shop, 500ft long × 200ft wide, opened in 1903, and the shell shop, built at
Government expense, and opened in 1915. The latter was taken over by the NER after
World War I and became No 2 Machine Shop. In 1912 a fine new office block was
built at Stooperdale to accommodate the chief mechanical engineer and his staff, with
nearby a new boiler shop and a new paint shop. The works closed in April 1966 but
attempts to set up an industrial estate using the old buildings do not seem to have met
with much success.

LOCOMOTION *(bottom right)*
S & D Crossing at Darlington with *Locomotion* standing on the line from Shildon,
and Pacific *Dick Turpin* passing on an up express. The photograph is a fake.

LOCOMOTION *Page 68 (top left)*
At first *Locomotion* was the only locomotive owned by the S & D, although a similar locomotive was on order and was delivered on 1 November 1825. The original engine, not named at first, was ordered from Robert Stephenson & Co. on 16 September 1824 and it was delivered exactly a year later, eleven days before the opening of the line on 27 September 1825. In January 1856 the company was about to sell *Locomotion* but at the last minute it was decided to preserve the engine and it was withdrawn from the sale. It was overhauled at Shildon works and then placed on a pedestal outside North Road station, where it remained for thirty-five years. In 1892 it was moved to Bank Top station, Darlington, where it could stand under cover.

LOCOMOTION *(bottom left)*
Both *Locomotion* and *Derwent* were removed to North Road Works, Darlington, in March 1961 for a complete overhaul. Fortunately photopraphs were taken of the engines stripped down, showing details of their construction not normally visible. This view shows the flat section eccentric rod from the leading axle, and the circular section rod for the rear valve, which obtained its motion by means of a bell-crank. In this case, as Brian Reed has pointed out, the bell-crank has been assembled in an incorrect position!

LOCOMOTION *Page 69 (top)*
This view of *Locomotion* shows the plates rivetted to the boiler by which the engine was supported on the axles.

DERWENT *Page 70*
Here *Derwent* is being re-assembled. The weatherboard has been fitted, together with the polished dome cover and the chimney. Note the different cylinder end covers.

DERWENT *Page 71*
The firehole of *Derwent* can just be seen under the inverted-U of the smokebox. Being a return-tube engine the fireman fired from the smokebox end of the locomotive, with the driver at the opposite end. The ends of the return tubes can be seen in the smokebox. Chimney (right) and dome cover (left) ready for re-assembly.

S & D Crossing 1965 *Page 72*
A more recent view of S & D Crossing near Darlington. Compare it with the one on page 67. This photograph shows LNER Class K4 2-6-0 No 3442 *The Great Marquess* as restored for preservation heading an enthusiasts special on the S & D line as it crosses the East Coast main line on 10 April 1965.

DERWENT *Page 74 (top left)*
The locomotive *Derwent*, built by Kitching & Co of Darlington in 1845. was sold to Pease & Partners for use on their colliery lines after it had been withdrawn in 1869. In 1898 it was presented to the NER for preservation and after restoration it joined *Locomotion* at Bank Top station, Darlington. This engine actually ran under its own steam in the 1925 Railway Centenary procession!

1925 CENTENARY CELEBRATIONS *(bottom left)*
For the S & D centenary in 1925 the LNER made elaborate preparations and arranged a procession of fifty-three old and modern locomotives from Stockton to Darlington. A large exhibition of locomotives and rolling stock, together with numerous small items of historic railway interest, was also held at Darlington in the newly completed Faverdale wagon works. Unfortunately it was not possible to hold the procession on the actual anniversary date, 27 September, because it was desired to allow it to be seen by the delegates attending the International Railway Congress, the meetings of which had been arranged to take place in Great Britain in early July. Thus the procession took place on 2 July 1925.

Page 75 (top)
The largest NER passenger class, the Raven Pacific design, was represented by 2400 *City of Newcastle*, hauling a train of new coaches for the Flying Scotsman express between London and Edinburgh. A number of lucky schoolchildren from Stockton were given a ride in the train as it slowly proceeded from Stockton to Fighting Cocks as the penultimate exhibit in the procession, and the dining cars in the train provided lunch for the 'artistes' who had travelled behind *Locomotion* in the replica train, dressed in period costume. Here the train is seen passing the grandstand at Goosepool.

1925 CENTENARY CELEBRATIONS *Page 76*
Large passenger engines were on show from the four main line companies, and there was also a display of some heavy freight engines, including Gresley's new 2-8-2 and Garratt locomotives. However, the North Eastern was not forgotten and included were such stalwarts as 0-8-0 engines of classes T1 and T3, and this P2 0-6-0.

Page 77 (top right)
Locomotion and replica train filled with passengers in period costume approaching the Grandstand as the last exhibit in the Centenary procession on 2 July 1925.

(bottom right)
It was the last item in the procession that was the pièce de résistance — *Locomotion* trundling slowly along, with its motion beams rhythmically rising and falling, hauling a train of chaldron wagons and the Directors' coach, all filled with men and women in period costume. The train was brought to a halt in front of the Grandstand, and started off again with a sudden jerk, causing many of the passengers to lose their balance, to the amusement of the spectators. On this occasion *Locomotion* was powered by a petrol engine in the tender, and oily waste was burned in the firebox to provide black smoke from the chimney!

PRESS ONLY

1275 AT MALTON *Page 78*

The long-boilered 0-6-0 1275 was actually built in the days when the S & D had been taken over by the NER but was still administered by the Darlington Committee, which continued many S & D practices, Thus the design was based on one which had proved economical to run, and which had evolved from a long line of 0-6-0 mineral engines on the S & D. No 1275 was one of a batch of ten from Dubs & Co of Glasgow, built in May and June 1874. It was reboilered in August 1883, June 1896, and September 1910 (second hand) and withdrawn from service in February 1923. It was the sole survivor of a batch of Class 1001 engines which had been stationed at Malton for working goods traffic on the Whitby branch: in 1922 this class and the McDonnell engines of Class 59 were the only 0-6-0 engines allowed on the branch. During its life No 1275 ran 907,341 miles.

1275 RESTORED *Page 79*
Fortunately 1275 was not scrapped after it had been withdrawn and it was put on one side for restoration, so that it could take part in the 1925 Centenary procession. After the procession it was one of the exhibits of locomotives and rolling stock at Faverdale wagon works, and it subsequently found a home in the Railway Museum at York. The work of restoring 1275 to its original condition was carried out at North Road works. Here it is standing outside the paint shop.

2-4-0 No 1068 *Page 80*
In 1875 the NER celebrated the fiftieth anniversary of the opening of the S & D by an exhibition of locomotives at North Road works. *Locomotion* was there, supported a few inches above the rails and connected to the shop's steam supply so that the wheels could revolve slowly. There was also a display of old and new engines; most of the latter had been specially painted for the occasion and carried the letters NER, which were not normally displayed on North Eastern engines at that time. No 1068 was built at Darlington in August 1875, only a few weeks before the Railway Jubilee Exhibition took place.

2-4-0 No 910 *Page 81*
Although most of the engines on display at North Road in 1875 were Stockton &
Darlington engines there were examples of locomotives built at Gateshead works and
by contractors, as well as some from other railway companies. To represent Gateshead
passenger engine practice 2-4-0 No 910 was chosen: at that time this was the largest
North Eastern passenger engine and locomotives of this type were used on the East
Coast expresses between York and Edinburgh. Fifty years later a few survivors of the
class could be seen at work on the former S & D line over the Pennines from Darlington
to Tebay.

HEIGHINGTON *Page 82*

Heighington, originally known as Aycliffe Lane, is where *Locomotion* was put on the rails after being transported from Newcastle by road in September 1825. A low cobbled section adjacent to the station buildings is thought to be part of the original platform, although the date of this is unknown. Locomotives commenced working the passenger coaches between Darlington and Shildon in December 1833: previously a service had been provided by horse-drawn vehicles.

Page 83
The station buildings, which carried the number plaque G2, are situated on falling ground and although only one storey high at the side facing the track, are actually two storeys high at the rear: thus the offices are on the upper floor as viewed from the back. Alterations have been made to the building in fairly recent times as the doorway shewn in the illustration opposite was originally a window. Previously the door was situated where the window is, in the corner of the building, to the left of the two posters.

WEST AUCKLAND *Page 84 (top left)*
The station at West Auckland did not show any signs of real antiquity, although for long the terminus of the passenger service. Probably all that was provided originally was a small building for the clerk, in which the passengers were allowed to wait in bad weather. It could be that improvements were carried out when the service between Bishop Auckland and Barnard Castle was introduced in 1863.

WEST AUCKLAND *(bottom left)*
The main item of interest at West Auckland was the station layout: this was unusual in that although there were two platforms they both faced the same way. At the south end of the station the original route of 1825 over the Brusselton inclines, was joined by the Tunnel branch of 1856, put in to avoid the inclines. At the north end of the station the original line continued up Etherley south incline, with what was originally the Haggerleases branch swinging away to the west. The station lost its goods facilities in 1958 and passenger traffic was withdrawn in 1962. Since then the site has been cleared except for the stationmaster's house.

BARNARD CASTLE *Page 85*
The Darlington & Barnard Castle Railway was opened in 1856 but when the line to Tebay was built it was impossible to continue the line westwards from the original station. Thus the new line had to branch off outside the Darlington & Barnard Castle station, which was left at the end of a spur and subsequently used as the goods station. The new station on the Tebay line was of the usual S & D single platform design, with an overall roof to the train shed, and it became an important junction station, with lines to Darlington and Bishop Auckland diverging at the east end of the station, and to Kirkby Stephen and Middleton in Teesdale at the west end. The yard on the north side handled the mineral trains in both directions over Stainmore. The station was closed to passenger traffic in November 1964 and has since been demolished.

TUNNEL JUNCTION *Page 86*
According to British Railways the building in the photograph was the ticket office at
Tunnel Junction. A station of sorts existed there — at the north end of Shildon tunnel —
from 1858 to 1863 to provide facilities for passengers changing from Darlington–Bishop
Auckland trains into trains on the West Auckland (St Helen's) and Haggerleases branch.
The connection between Tunnel Junction and West Auckland had been built to by-pass
the Brusselton inclines. The station became redundant with the opening of a direct line
from Bishop Auckland to West Auckland in 1863 in conjunction with the line to Barnard
Castle.

KIRKBY STEPHEN *Page 87*

The line over Stainmore summit was opened in 1861 and Kirkby Stephen became an important intermediate station between Darlington and Tebay. The station differed from the usual S & D design in having an island platform, with access from the road bridge across the line at the east end of the station. A covered way ran from the overbridge, down the steps, and along the platform to the station buildings. For many years the luggage was taken up and down between the bridge and the platform by an electric lift and for many years the electricity for the lift, the station lighting, and machines in the locomotive shed, was supplied by a water turbine generator powered by the nearby River Eden. Each platform was covered by a canopy stretching from the station buildings to a row of iron columns outside the tracks, but these columns imposed a restricted clearance and they were replaced by walls set further out in 1883.

STAINMORE SUMMIT *Page 88*

The South Durham & Lancashire Union Railway was one of the lines nominally built by a separate company, but the S & D was behind it and worked the line from its opening between Barnard Castle and Tebay in August 1861. The line crossed the top of the Pennines, spurning a tunnel, but taking advantage of a small pass in the hills at Stainmore summit, 1,370ft above sea level. It is a line which aroused a lot of interest, probably because of its operating difficulties and scenic beauty. Like most lines traversing high ground the upper reaches of the line were susceptible to heavy snowfalls and drifting, which could put the line out of action for weeks.

Stockton TO Darlington.	Stockton TO Darlington.
No. Second Class, 1 6	No. Second Class, 1 6
day of 184	day of 184
Please to hold this Ticket till called for.	Please to hold this Ticket till called for.
Stockton TO Darlington.	Stockton TO Darlington.
No. Second Class, 1 6	No. Second Class, 1 6
day of 184	day of 184
Please to hold this Ticket till called for.	Please to hold this Ticket till called for.
Stockton TO Darlington.	Stockton TO Darlington.
No. Second Class, 1 6	No. Second Class, 1 6
day of 184	day of 184
Please to hold this Ticket till called for.	Please to hold this Ticket till called for.

STOCKTON & DARLINGTON RAILWAY CO.

RAILWAY EXCURSIONS.

THE COMPANY HAVE BUILT A HANDSOME

SALOON CARRIAGE,

FOR THE USE OF

PLEASURE PARTIES,

WHICH MAY BE ENGAGED FOR THE DAY ON THE FOLLOWING TERMS:—

	12 Miles and Back.			24 Miles and back.		
	£	s.	d.	£	s.	d.
Not exceeding 12 passengers, - -	2	2	0	3	3	0
„ 18 „ - -	3	3	0	4	10	0

APPLICATION FOR THE SAME TO BE MADE TO MR. GEORGE STEPHENSON, RAILWAY STATION, DARLINGTON.

Railway Office, Darlington, August, 1855.

HARRISON PENNEY, PRINTER, DARLINGTON.

TICKETS *Page 90 (top left)*
Paper tickets printed in sheets of ten were used until the 1840s. Each ticket was approximately 4in × 2½in, of coloured paper with black lettering. The Stockton to Darlington tickets were white; Fighting Cocks to St Helen's were blue; and Middlesbrough to Yarm were green.

SALOON CARRIAGE *(bottom left)*
The notice advertising the Saloon Carriage for pleasure parties is dated August 1855. The George Stephenson mentioned on the notice was the traffic manager of the S & D, not the famous locomotive engineer and railway builder.

1925 CENTENARY MEDALLION *Page 91 (top)*
To commemorate the centenary of the S & D in 1925 the LNER commissioned a medallion depicting on one side the busts of Edward Pease and George Stephenson, together with the arms of the towns of Stockton and Darlington: on the reverse was the figure of Vulcan, holding in his hand *Locomotion*, with a Gresley Pacific locomotive in the background. This bronze medallion, designed by Gilbert Bayes, was issued in two sizes, 1¾in and 3in diameter at 5s 0d and 10s 0d respectively. Profits were donated to the Railway Benevolent Institution.

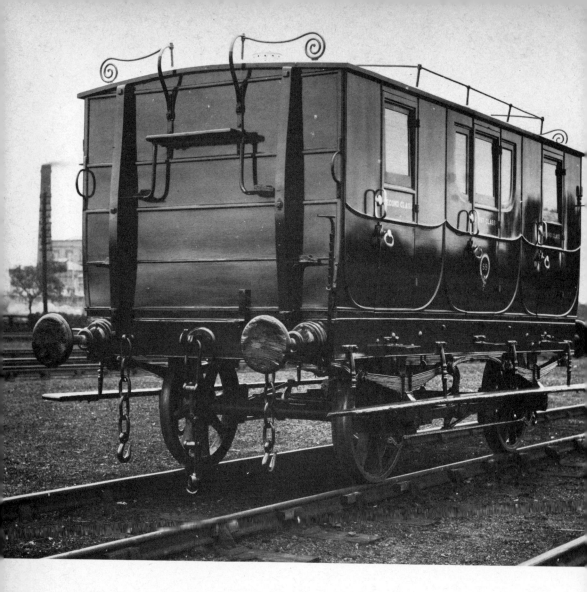

FIRST- AND SECOND-CLASS COACH *Page 92*
Unfortunately little is known about S & D coaches, and few photographs of them exist.
The NER did, however, preserve some four-wheel composite coaches dating from the
1840s. These have three compartments, second-class at each end and a first-class in the
centre. The second-class compartments had only the upper part of the door glazed
whereas the first-class had a glazed quarter light on each side of the door. Rails and
tarpaulins were provided for the luggage carried on the roof, and a guard's seat was also
fitted on the roof.

SMOKING CARRIAGE *Page 93*
The S & D built an elaborate composite smoking carriage in 1870, also on four wheels, with a second-class compartment at each end and a first-class saloon in the centre. The wheelbase was 15ft and the body was 27ft 6in long and 7ft 10in wide. Each compartment was 5ft 6in wide and the first saloon was 15ft 7$\frac{1}{2}$in long, seating six passengers down each side, three on each side of the door. The saloon section was surmounted by a clerestory 7in high, on which were mounted elaborate ventilators according to the official drawing, but these do not appear on the photograph above.

NORTH ROAD DRINKING FOUNTAIN *Page 94*
Facing the main entrance to North Road station was a drinking fountain provided by the railway company. Behind the fountain originally ran the Darlington Depots branch but in later years the area was occupied by the locomotive scrap yard.

INDEX